# STILL A PC

*Also by Bill Stone
and published by
Gwenstone Publications:*

A Feral Cat Dies in Beirut
Forty Odd Years On
One Act Play

*Also by Bill Stone
and published by
Citizen Publications:*

The Virgin and the Shadow
Dead Fishes
God Is a Nigger

# STILL A POET AT 80?

## Bill Stone

*with contributions by*

## Yasmin Hussein

Gwenstone Publications

First edition published by Gwenstone Publications
Flat 1, Highcliffe Court, 35 Cheriton Gardens,
Folkestone, Kent CT20 2AP
email: recluse6@msn.com

Copyright (c) 2019 Bill Stone

The right of Bill Stone to be identified as the author of this work has been asserted in accordance with sections 77 and 78 of the copyright designs and Patents Act 1988.

A catalogue record of this book is available from the British Library.

First edition 2019

*Condition of sale:*
All Rights Reserved. No part of this publication may be reproduced, stored in a retrieval system or transmitted in any form or by any means, electronic, mechanical, photocopying, recording, scanning or otherwise, except under the terms of the Copyright, Designs and Patents Act 1988 or under the terms of a licence issued by the Copyright Licensing Agency Ltd, 90 Tottenham Court Road, London W1T 4LP, UK, without the permission in writing of the Publisher.

ISBN: 978-0-9552976-2-5

# CONTENTS

*About the Author*     9
*Foreword*     11

**Forty Odd Years On**     17
Prologue     19
An Earthly Life Begins     23
The End of an Earthly Life     25
For My Young Friend Monika     26
I Am Alone     27
Haunted     28
This Ghost     30
This Moth     31
Visitors     32

**Palestine**     33
Palestine     35
Thoraya     37

**The Virgin and the Shadow**     39
The Virgin and the Shadow     41
Astral Nightmare     42
A Poet Said It     43
Life Is a Kaleidoscope     44
Pleading for Recognition     45
And Yet I Love Her     46
My Dog     48
Atomic Poem Two     49
A Poet at the Crucifixion     50
For Mary Ann (A Child)     51

| | |
|---|---|
| The Summer Rose | 52 |
| A Poet's Denunciation | 53 |
| Minute Penned Thoughts | 54 |
| Clearness of Vision | 56 |
| Futility | 57 |
| Writing Then Is Like Talking | 58 |
| Epitaph | 59 |
| | |
| **Dead Fishes** | **61** |
| Dead Fishes | 63 |
| A Poem for the Freedom from Hunger Campaign | 64 |
| Ants | 65 |
| Imprisoned | 66 |
| Ants Again | 67 |
| Homosexual Temptation | 68 |
| Atomic Poem Three | 69 |
| Respectful Reply to Dom Silvester Houédard | 70 |
| A Question | 72 |
| Ghost Lights | 73 |
| Clarity with Death | 74 |
| Watching | 75 |
| Plain or Cheese and Onion? | 76 |
| Fog Telegraphy | 77 |
| | |
| **God Is a Nigger** | **81** |
| Modern Poetry | 83 |
| The Foreigner | 84 |
| Age | 85 |
| For the Dead Poets and Others | 87 |
| The Shadow | 88 |
| Years Later… | 89 |
| Movie | 90 |
| Lament of a Young Poet | 91 |

| | |
|---|---|
| Thoughts in a Chinese Restaurant | 92 |
| For Danielle | 93 |
| For Eileen | 94 |
| God Is a Nigger | 95 |
| Mary Jane | 96 |
| Message for a Child | 98 |
| Untitled Poems | 99 |
| Poem 1 | 99 |
| Poem 2 | 99 |
| Poem 3 | 100 |
| Poem 4 | 100 |
| Poem 5 | 101 |
| Poem 6 | 101 |
| Bizarre Thoughts | 102 |
| Two Concrete Poems | 104 |
| Dedication | 104 |
| Concrete Poem 1: The Paper Boy | 105 |
| Concrete Poem 2: Farewell Departed Wife and Friends | 106 |
| **Lebanon Inspired Poems *by Yasmin Hussein*** | **107** |
| The Beauty of Lebanon | 109 |
| Secrets | 110 |
| The Voice | 111 |
| The Sandman | 112 |
| Home Sweet Home | 113 |
| The Meaning of Life | 114 |
| Like a Stone | 115 |
| The Train Ride | 116 |
| **Lebanon Inspired Poems *by Bill Stone*** | **117** |
| Thoughts on Christmas Day | 119 |
| Untitled Lebanon Poems | 120 |
| Thoughts | 123 |

| | |
|---|---|
| Sick Humour? | 124 |
| A Beggar's Dog | 125 |
| I Saw a Sad Dog! | 126 |
| Slow Is the Snail | 127 |
| Maybe? | 128 |
| An Anatomy of Idiosyncrasies | 129 |

**The Not So Grim Reaper – *A One-Act Play***    **131**

| | |
|---|---|
| That's All Now Folks | 151 |
| Appendix: British Airways competition poems: | |
|   *Debra Stone and Ray Hatcher* | 153 |
| Conclusion | 159 |
| *Index* | 161 |

# ABOUT THE AUTHOR

WILLIAM LAWRENCE STONE was born 21 April 1939 in Leatherhead, Surrey. His father William was conscripted for the duration of the Second World War, leaving his mother Ruth with a five-month-old baby. She then moved with Bill to Swanscombe, Kent to live with her parents. Bill's granddad's harsh regime of beatings with a leather belt were frequent, even for minor childish misdemeanours.

When his father was demobbed Bill went back to living with his parents in a prefab. Sadly his mother became ill and died in 1948 and within a short period of time his father's new 'woman' came to live with them. In a state of rebellion, and fuelled by a sense of rejection and resentment, Bill returned to his grandparents' home, where his granddad continued with his harsh regime, Bill having by now become a member of a local boxing club where Dave Charnley, European Lightweight Champion, was also a member. Between the ages of 16 and 17 Bill ran away to join the Merchant Navy, eventually becoming an engineer officer. In his subsequent career, returning to sea was always an option.

At 21 Bill joined the Royal Engineers and was posted to Fleet Hants training camp to find that Corporal Dave Charnley was doing his National Service as a physical training instructor. This influenced Bill's decision to join the regiment's boxing team. During training he visited Farnborough Abbey, a Benedictine monastery, and met Dom Silvester Houédard, forming a lifelong friendship with him, as well as being introduced by the latter to the world of poetry.

Bill discovered his spiritual home in Paris in the 1960s. He was introduced to Dom Silvester's connections, including many writers, and often stayed at the famous bookshop Shakespeare and Co. in Paris. Returning to sea proved a constant escape route. Bill's occupations have included: soldier, seaman, publican and international security operative. As for other professional activities, he comments, 'I'd have to shoot you if I told you.'

From schooldays when he created and edited a school magazine, Bill has had a continued interest in writing and has been in several war zones including the Algerian War of Independence in Oran, 1962, witnessing the ending of hostilities; Iran, witnessing the demise of the Shah in the 1970s and the return of Ayatollah Khomeini from exile in Paris; and with his family experiencing conflict in Lebanon.

In Capetown, South Africa at the Monastery Hospital he received the Last Rites as he was not expected to survive treatment for malignant malaria and black water fever. He has also survived a heart attack and bowel cancer, and arriving in Agadir was stricken by a devastating earthquake on 29 February 1960.

Bill stood for Parliament in Dover as an Independent Social Democrat supported by Dick Taverne, the former Labour MP who joined the SDP before becoming a Liberal Democrat. Over the years Bill has attended associate meetings in the House of Commons and support from Members. He is a Fellow of the British Institute of Innkeepers, Member of the International Professional Security Association, Member of the Palestine Solidarity campaign and Co-Founder of the National Pubwatch a police partnership to combat alcohol-related crime and disorder.

# FOREWORD

*Acknowledging Dom Sylvester Houédard*

IN MY BOOK of verse *God Is a Nigger*, published in 1964, there is a poem called 'Age'. Over fifty-five years later I am reflecting the irony of growing old. This poses a self-question, 'Where in my younger days did this profound vision of old age stem?' My contemplations seem to enhance a perception of parallel worlds and previous earthly incarnations.

Dom Sylvester Houédard, a Benedictine monk from Prinknash Abbey, was my literary mentor and friend and reviewed my poems in the *Aylesford Review*, published by the Carmelite community at the Aylesford Priory in Kent, edited by Fr Brocard Sewell. He wrote 'Stone, a young Catholic poet concerned about the "In/outsideness of life", is a poet at twenty is a poet at forty.'

Both Dom Sylvester and Fr Brocard Sewell were icons in the world of literature.

Gerveys Sewell (1912–2000), usually now known by his religious name Brocard Sewell, was a British Carmelite friar and literary figure.

He was born in Bangkok, and brought up in Cornwall, England. Educated at Weymouth College (leaving at 16), he became a Catholic convert in 1931. As a young man he was involved with H. D. C. Pepler in craft printing, before testing his vocation first of all with the Dominicans, whom he left shortly before joining the Royal Air Force during World War II. Returning after the war to religious life, he was professed first of all with the Austin Canons before becoming a Carmelite friar in 1952 (and being ordained priest in 1954), remaining with the Carmelites for the rest of his life.

In a subsequent career as editor, publisher, printer and writer, he commemorated and wrote up a number of lesser literary lights: Arthur Machen, Frederick Rolfe, Montague Summers, Marc-André Raffalovich, John Gray, Olive Custance, Henry Williamson. He also wrote on distributist figures and the Eric Gill and Ditchling circle. Using the *Aylesford Review* – the magazine of the monastery in which he was cloistered – he also publicised the works of some of the 1960s counterculture poets, in particular Michael Horovitz and his erstwhile wife Frances Horovitz, who with others made many trips to Aylesford Priory during the 1960s and 1970s. Sewell, who enjoyed a close friendship with Frances Horovitz, became her confessor and confidant (the fact that she was not Roman Catholic did not prevent Sewell hearing her confession) and following her death of cancer in 1983, he became her biographer

Dom Sylvester Houedard (1924–92), or DSH, as he is correctly known, was a Benedictine monk of Prinknash Abbey, Gloucestershire, who made significant contributions in many fields, including theology and poetry.

DSH was born in Guernsey in 1924, and educated at Jesus College, Oxford, 1942–44 and 1947–49, and at St Anselmo, Rome, 1951–55. Between 1944 and 1947 he served in British Army intelligence. In 1949, he became a monk at Prinknash Abbey, Gloucestershire, and he entered the priesthood in 1959. He made major contributions to theology and, inspired by the Second Vatican Council, became a luminary in the ecumenical movement. DSH was particularly respected for his work with the Ibn 'Arabi Society and with Buddhist scholars. He was also renowned as a translator of religious texts, in 1962 he published his translation of the Office of Our Lady and he played a leading role in the Jerusalem Bible translation of 1961 in the capacity of literary editor for the New Testament and sub-editor for the Old Testament.

However DSH was best-known as an outstanding exponent of 'concrete poetry' (visual poetry). He invented the 'typestract', a form of poem that took up the pattern making possibilities of the typewriter. His visual poetries were frequently exhibited both at home and abroad. His most famous celebrated poem was 'Frog-pond-plop', a translation from the Japanese haiku of Matsuo Basho (1644–94), which he presented in the form of an opening poem following an origami unfolding principle. Although considered avant-garde, DSH considered he was also continuing long-standing poetic traditions of the Benedictine order. He corresponded widely with leading poets, artists, theologians and philosophers, and his address book was said to have contained 3,000 names.

As a child I felt a compulsion to explore that 'In/outsideness' of 'my' life with a feeling of alienation from what I felt was the perceived 'me'. This was confirmed when at junior school I glanced at a half-open swing type window and saw the reflection of a scenario happening some distance from my school. This infused me with a seeking for the perception of parallel existences.

A lasting inspiration for writing stems from witnessing the 'pangs of despised love' and man's inhumanity towards others, including animals, creatures, birds and nature. Therefore I dedicate this work to all victims of crimes on Earth against humanity and nature, the perpetrators' retribution established in a godless eternity where their sprits may dwell.

*Bill Stone with his granddaughter, Yasmin Hussein*

# FORTY ODD YEARS ON

**Bill Stone**

# PROLOGUE

AN OLD TREE stood alone in the shopping precinct. A young Turtle Dove perched between leaves supported by a thin stem protruding from a top branch. The Dove's eye view merged with an over-view of the tree world in which it took respite. With a compulsive urge I held my left hand on the tree trunk. With this action I psychologically felt an interfusion in time memory. An interface had been breached linking me with a seemingly enlightened spiritual knowledge of eternity.

The sun looking pale offered little heat to my body which already felt cold. A light breeze intensified the chill stunting my muse. I continued walking as the tree scene, now past tense, merged into history.

A shop window mirror image reflects activity of people out of direct vision. Customers swirling around the Pound Shop clutching purchases as if expecting the 'bargains' to be seized back. This parallel world opens around the next corner. If there is not a diversion, entry is inevitable. I hesitate, contemplating the choice: continue walking towards the Pound Shop or turn back towards Sainsbury's supermarket?

Sitting close by Sainsbury's entrance is a 'homeless' (?) beggar with a dejected-looking dog to encourage sympathy from compassionate passers-by.

Not far away a young girl is also begging. She sits cross-legged and alone on a dirty, worn blanket, embossed with the colours of a Scottish clan; she presents a sad victim with her hands outstretched, pleading for money. Compassionate donors are blissfully unaware that they also are contributing to her drug addiction.

The beggar girl starts to convulse. Her face distorted by pain. Nobody tries to help her. The excuses and comments are offered by a now gawking assembly:
'It's a junkie.'
'Don't know what contagious viruses she may have.'
'Call the police.'
'Don't touch her.'
'Somebody all an ambulance.'
'She's not moving.'
'She doesn't look right to me.'

The beggar girl began to convulse and then, emitting a final seizure, collapsed 'lifeless'. The babbling audience ceased to comment, leaving an uncanny silence. Then a hysterical gawker screamed an assumption, *'Oh God! She's dead!'*

The beggar's life had ended. She was now another historic event to be documented in the next edition of the local Gazette:

HEROIN ADDICT DIES BEGGING
ON SAINSBURYS DOORSTEP

The young Turtle Dove from the tree flight, tired, huddles exhausted kerbside of a zebra crossing and falls off the kerb; fortunately the lights are on red. Now it snuggles peacefully cupped in its rescuer's hands, weak but not injured, the surmised epitaph being:

If the rescuer had continued
to turn the corner towards the Pound Shop...

If the beggar girl had not died
causing him to pause for a short while...
Events would have changed
and the Turtle Dove may not have been saved.

# AN EARTHLY LIFE BEGINS

*A baby boy becomes...*

*a young man ...*

*becomes a middle aged man...*

*becomes an old man...*

*awaiting*

# THE END OF AN EARTHLY LIFE

'Then is now
Now is then tomorrow
Gone is then
A signet becomes a swan
The signet has gone
Whilst a lamb becomes a sheep
Now the lamb has gone.'

Whilst love and
Dreams have passed away
A faded memory of yesterday.

## FOR MY YOUNG FRIEND MONIKA

I will never regret that you entered my life.
But
You disturbed my mind,
Disrupted my thoughts
Causing me to envy youth.
I wish that you could linger a while
Whilst I continue to appreciate your company.

You are beautiful
Your personality is a stimulant
An encouragement to enjoy life.

You and I are just passing
Pausing whilst I steal a little of your charm
I am content to accept that a
Pleasant thought of you will last forever
Wherever you are
To recall when sadly memories
Are all that I have.

# I AM ALONE

There is nobody there, never is.
Just another noise, a disturbance.
Footsteps filter in from another place,
A distant voice echoes.

It continues again and again.
Followed by creaking floorboard
Now a shadow passes?

Mad! I'm going mad!
Another sound, more footsteps
Perhaps someone really is coming.
Is it a stranger, a visitor, company?

I do not even recognise myself.
I am still alone.
The voice is mine, the 'visitor' is my reflection.

# HAUNTED

I am haunted; my soul is captured
In a shell that is not mine
A distant whisper calls, urging escape.
Escape?
An indistinguishable voice is
Trying to awake my forgotten world.

Alone I speak to a myriad of images
Historical memories comfort a splitting mind,
An intrusive statement that I still exist.

Squealing and moaning images pass in and out.
Ghouls from some lesser world?
I have no affinity with them
THEY ARE NOT MY BUSINESS!
I am my business
History is my co-existence
The dilemma is not my fault.
I am a trapped victim of inhumanity.
Escape is not impossible.
There are no locked doors, no chains and no guards.

Why am I unable then to walk away?
Just leave.
No questions asked
No reclamations
Freedom awaits.
There is no prison

There are no walls
*BECAUSE*
I AM THE PRISON
AND
THE PRISONER
What then would freedom be?
Another prison, I suspect.
Again trapped by insane rejects.
Talking gibberish,
Demanding my attention
Storming my mind
Leaving no space for me!

# THIS GHOST

This ghost, this ex person
Does not disturb me.
Doesn't worry me
Don't interfere with my sanity.
It goes about its business
Wandering here and there,
It does not invade my space or demand attention.
She stops at an imposed interface
By mutual agreement.
She has a beautiful face that radiates serenity,
Which I would welcome into my heart
If she were real.
But
She is following a different route
I have to go my way
She has to go her way.
Both locked in parallel passages
Together yet infinitely apart.

# THIS MOTH

This moth, so big.
Lost
Trapped in my cell
Flying in frightened frenzy
Seeking a way out of its hell.
'Try to catch when still, try to help
When most would kill.'
'It's huge the biggest one
That I have ever seen
And adorned with a gorgeous hue.'
Nervous when touched.
Hands closing in like great shovels as such.
Gently trapped, the terrified creature
Must think in a final shroud it is now wrapped.
Released it flies high
Soaring over the trees
It's free, it's free every bird cries.
I too am excited insane.
'THE MOTH'S SAVIOUR'
Then I realise that I am alone again.

# VISITORS

They promise to return
Those visitors to my dreams
But they never do
Only strangers curious, unfriendly
Turning sweet dreams into a nightmare.
I wait for the others, the friendly ones.
Hoping, watching, needing their company
Turning desperate for any company.

A voice in the night 'someone to hold?'
To convince my troubled spirit
That I am not alone and the world still exists.
Far from here maybe but not yet lost.
Hoping that it awaits my return.
A final visit maybe?
To say goodbye from those who remember me,
But sadly not to know me.
Nobody will ever know me.

# PALESTINE

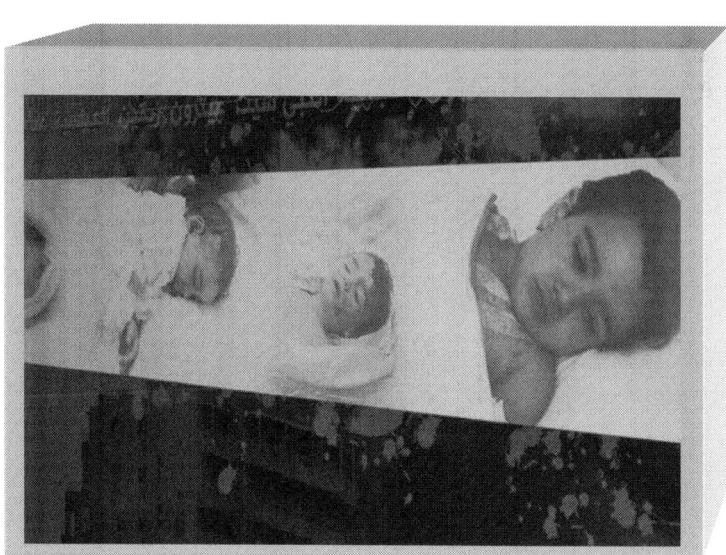

# PALESTINE

'APOLOGY TO THE VICTIMS'
FOR THE
SLICES OF FLESH
AN ARM, A LEG OR GAUGED OUT EYES
SCATTERED IN A BLOODY INTERMIX.
A HEAD OR FEET EVEN FEATHERS
FROM THE CHILDRENS PET CHICKS'
AS ALWAYS
A DOLLY, TEDDY AND OTHER LOVED TOYS

AND OF COURSE
A RAT OR TWO!
THIS CARNAGE, THIS WASTE OF LIFE
IS NOT JUST THE DEMOLITION
OF A REGIME?
THE DEAD
NOT TYRANTS, DESPOTS OR PERSECUTORS
NOT PRESIDENTS, PRIME MINISTERS,
GENERALS
OR IMPERIALISTIC MOGULS.
THE DEAD NOT
ANYTHING POWERFUL OR FISCAL.
NO!
JUST FAMILIES. JUST SOLDIERS,
**JUST PEOPLE**
**MUSLIMS**
**CHRISTIANS**
**JEWS**
**BUDDHISTS**
**HINDUS**

'SORRY YOU ARE DEAD. SORRY THAT THE
SOLDIERS ARE DEAD TOO.
SORRY, SORRY SO SORRY
**BUT**
WE ARE STILL PROUD
TO HAVE **LIBERATED** YOU.
SO REST IN INNOCENCE PEACE
WITH YOUR GOD

WHILST
**OURS STRUGGLE TO PREVENT ITS TAIL
BECOMING IMPALED ON ITS HORNS!**

# THORAYA

There you are isolated in a war
**VIOLENCE!**
Not your fault. Nothing you can do.
**VICTIM!**
Witness death, seeing children slaughtered!
**ALONE!**
A young beautiful covered Muslim,
graduate with distinction
**UNFAIR!**
A commodity in the imperialistic world.
'Ignore the suffering, ignore the killing,'
Get stuffed with

**MACDONALDS
KENTUCKY FRIED
COCA COLA**

(Their profits feed the war machine.)
**LIFE passes by** and your sun never sets.
**SADNESS!**
That haunting smile, those lovely eyes
**REMAIN**
THE PERPRETRATORS KNOW OF THEIR
COLLECTIVE GUILT!
**CRUEL!**
Live on lovely, defy their devils.
**MESSENGER!**
For others weaker see your courage
**REDEEMER!**

Every dead eye
Every severed limb
**MENDING!**
In a place beyond your hell.
**SATAN!**
In the guise of politicians
**WATCHING!**
Distant yet spiritually close a friend
**REACHING!**
Unconditional growing compassion.
**MANIPULATED!**
A selfish world unable to change.
It is not yours or mine
We retreat into our own space
Beyond reach
Silent witnesses of their crimes against humanity.

# THE VIRGIN
# AND
# THE SHADOW

*Poems by*
*William L. Stone*

Citizen Publications
Southend-on-Sea

ONE SHILLING AND SIXPENCE
Published 1964

# THE VIRGIN AND THE SHADOW

She dreams, her virgin soul awaken
To the urgent desires of life.
(Which she dare feel only in sleep)
How her young breast is dented
Snuggled in her dream lover's arm.
The silent shadow beside her bed
Steal a gentle kiss.
The yoke of her waking body
Stirs with sweet expectancy
But the shadow is not a thief
(Thank God)
Yet his smooth fingers burn
Throbbing with shame as he
Touched the richness of her body.
Invading her innocence.
Now crying the dewy tears of dawn.
Choking with the passion of illicit thoughts
He fades as his desired love awakes still a virgin.

## ASTRAL NIGHTMARE

Shadowy spirits around me.
*Severed limbs, butchered corpses of reeking flesh,*
**I fear you not!**
This astral life I ventured escaping the pain of love.
So let your bloody trails lead where they may.
I will follow relentlessly seeking retribution
For that nothing I had in life.
Headless body passing by
I have no fear of you.
Such an appalling abomination
Cannot hurt me more that she.
Green grinning head
Fire spitting eyes!
**Make way!** before I trample you under foot
As I seek to reunite her spirit and body

Horrors of this astral night
I hope that she's not here
But this I really know.
Seeking where she is not
Among all other dreams both vile and sweet
Is but a motive

To resist her warm earthly body
A screaming magnetic seduction
Promising love which will be poison for me.

## A POET SAID IT

'One day a poet will make a mistake
By writing so that others can understand.
Then the hidden skeletons in life
Will be **exposed!**'

# LIFE IS A KALEIDOSCOPE

This pain scatters blinding colours at my mind's eye,
Smashing skull deliberately against a brick wall
Comes the realisation that I am about to die.

Within a kaleidoscopic view is a fragment reflection
Of my love smiling in a white wedding dress.
Whilst a hated groom gloats over my rejection.

The black grim reaper driving his coach of death
Has no compassion for the cargo that is my soul.
The colours now scatter as I draw my final breath.
My life was just an insignificant stream
Of bubbling troubled love,
Regretting all the cruel words that I did not mean.

The coach of death passes by a Muslim girl
Crying and pleading 'Don't make me marry him'
As she too becomes cargo to love's hell.

Yahweh, Vishnu, Siddhartha, Jehovar, Allah or God
I plead with whoever you are.
Reveal your true form and lift this blinding fog.

# PLEADING FOR RECOGNITION

Chide
I cried
for a child
not my own
but like me
young alone
rejected
I pleaded
eyes I love
scorned
and still
virginal
God's will?

## AND YET I LOVE HER

If time is tired
Then so am I
For it was her breast I felt
To find a heart beating time to death.
And yet I love her
She is very young
But time is age
As she was just
Ten thousand years ago.
Perhaps it is her body
With screaming sex appeal?
How can that be
For I am disconnected
And yet I love her.
Perhaps that smile
In a deep cushioned eye
To snuggle my loneliness
But that eye
Still reflects her today
Seeing ten thousand others
A glance that sweeps a speck
That is me to her
Into a vacuum of nothing
And yet I love her.
If I were alive
Free from these chains
She would not know
Any love but mine
Lips soft and warm

## Still a Poet at 80?

Lay still and be happy
Alone with ten thousand others
And yet I love her.
Echo into space times is now
Should we make love
Hidden in the darkness?
To hate the stench
Of cruel odour that refuses freedom
Comes from the sweat of time
That's left a mark
Ten thousand marks in fact
And yet I love her.
Now to sadistic mutual death
To share one grave
Where now the beauty?
For what the desire?
Alone in a grave
With ten thousand others.

# MY DOG

If I could have a dog
To call my pal
And wander through the
Cloudy fields
Without a law to rule
Then my heart would be
Lightened after heavy love
With my dog and a field
Miles of nowhere to go
Drifting by dandelions
Shaking yellow heads
Laughing with my dog
And I
Knowing we are free
Without the bonded
Chains of her false love.

## ATOMIC POEM TWO

Lurking in the shadows
Crying to the night
Watching eyes unseen
Glows an orange light
Depths of evil hover
A virgin sound asleep
Pillowed sweet unknowing
Sex to yet discover
In-between the two
The wall of a poet
A Catholic God in hand
With a monastic friend
Leaning to the fall
Save us we plead
Deliver from evil
The sleeping virgin
A tired poet
And the holy monk.

## A POET AT THE CRUCIFIXION

Standing in the shadows
Of an age gone by
Watching as they crucified
A man who would not die.
He looked at me with sad eyes
That said 'I will forgive
For you are just a poet
Who has centuries to live.

# FOR MARY ANN (A CHILD)

On a stormy night from the bow of my ship
As you stroke my face with your windy breath
Inviting me into your arms of death
Treacherous beauty of the sea
Sleek as a panther waiting to strike
Cold as a mountain in nature's night
Plague of the sailor yet friend of a child.

## THE SUMMER ROSE

Full red with sensual burning
Beautiful rose of a summer's day
Velvet petals beneath my touch
Caressing hidden nipples of her breast
Swaying gentle in the breeze.
A lullaby in nature's garden.
Laying together sweet smelling day
Tactful creatures turn their heads.
Dear serenity of this Eden
Retreated from all worldly stench
To breathe between scented breasts
Cradled softly my lonely mind
Aching no more life's cruel way.
As my hand gently brushes her thigh
That madness of moment, the final blissful surge
As winter creeps lurking from the shadows.
Embarrassed poor rose of summer
Covers hastily in dull brown
Seen naked is now ashamed
Of her full red body
Which condemned a whore
From winter's hard eyes
Withers to die slowly and alone.

## A POET'S DENUNCIATION

Poetry is written by fools
For self-professed intellectuals.

# MINUTE PENNED THOUGHTS

~1~
Okay then look
Laugh at the poet
BUT
Stop laughing
Read
Live your life and die
And?
The poet lives on.

~2~
How's this for a poem
Four and twenty me's
Sitting in a pub
Thinking of just one you
Which leaves a moral of
You die, I die
And still four and twenty me's
Sit in a pub thinking of
ONE YOU!

~3~
Theological colours.
Green to purple or perhaps
Gold
Is that a mouse or red
She is not my love but
Blue
Black as anger

Evil painted
Brown
A devil of
Grey
Sweet love
White
Making love
Gold
Most beautiful intergraded
Black on white .

~4~
The typewriter and I
Words our common
Each one marks time
For me to die.

~5~
We kissed to say hello
And shook hands to say
Goodbye
For when we said hello
You were a child
But when we said
Goodbye
You were a woman
And a stranger.

## CLEARNESS OF VISION

Where are all the people
That I used to know
Seeing bodies like friends
Who speak a stranger's tongue
Gone familiar intimacies
Of the faithless days
Has a mist lifted
For me to clearly see
My friends as I should have
In my wasted youth.

## FUTILITY

People who live alone
Die alone
Those who live in words
Love alone
The artists and the painters
Create alone
And God laughs at us all.

# WRITING THEN IS LIKE TALKING

Writing then is like talking to one's self
Observers don't really want to know
They can see nobody listens
But excuse it for the spirit of youth
At the street corner, in the pictures
(Back row) or even in the cloakrooms
At school
After all it is only the spirit of youth
A promising reward for doing a ton?
For those who survive
Hoping to score where others didn't.
There are no sweet young girls today
Only birds, chicks, skirt and crumpet
Would you like to know what I think?
You have no choice silent paper
'I think the whole world suddenly changed
Because Satan changed the signpost.
So no more a of a choice of heaven or hell
Because we are all lost again in Eden.
Did they did press the button?
Now we are discovering sex all over again
The original sin?
(Don't eat the apple!)
Will God offer save us this time?
Hasn't he has enough to do
Dying and resurrecting every time
We make a mess of things
When all he wants is to show us real sex
That is often mistaken for love…

## EPITAPH

When I am dead
Should my words live on
Think on me as
A bygone you
Loving the same old way
Crying the same old tears
And dying in the fall.

# DEAD FISHES

*Poems by*

WILLIAM L. STONE

*For Gran who is dead*

Citizen Publishing
Southend-on-Sea

Published 1964

# DEAD FISHES

Like the time I saw fishes
Floating sideways in silvery death
After a small boy had speared
Them with a fork tied to a stick
Then the sadistic little mind
Urinated in the blood mixed water
Arriving home he called his granny
A fat old cow
When caught stealing sixpence
From her purse
After which for spite he tied two
Cats together by their tails
And hung them over the wash line
Then went to collect his choir pay
From the vicar
From where he left with an innocent
Smile
Stepped from the curb right under a
Bus
And like the fishes floated sideway
Quite dead.

## A POEM FOR THE FREEDOM FROM HUNGER CAMPAIGN
*(written on Christmas Day)*

There are others now whose only luxury is
A cigarette picked from the gutter,
And children who cry instead of laugh at Christmas
Whilst my friends throw grapes
At each other for fun,
Or pour wine over the drunkard's head.
There are children whose scabby legs
And sunken eyes
Need only food,
Yet my kid brother chooses carefully his sweets.
Then the lovers who never go to bed together
Weak from starvation, preoccupied with worry,
Ironically my friend paid a prostitute for 'love'
There will be starving dying people this Christmas,
But why should we care there are peaches with our
PHEASANT ON CHRISTMAS DAY!

# ANTS

There are the great ants who rule
With a code of ruthless contempt
Without moral considerations.
Their crocodile tears run down cheeks of gold
Each will cost a man his pride.
Then there are the small ants,
Who scurry in a mass with tiny
Fears and invited problems.
Not one attracts a sympathetic thought
Beyond the barrier of the great ants arrogance.
Then there are the apathetic zombie ants
Who wander in fantasy among the
Ruins of civilisation
Hoping something still exists.
Not caring make the zombie ants
A constant worry to the great ants.
Then there are the sex ants
Who supply the ranks of all,
Wandering freely giving freely to
The great, the little and zombie alike.
With cunning manipulation rule the great ants.
Then there are the trained ants,
Pawns behind the gun,
Fired by the great ants.
Who destroy without reason, all ants.
So ants this pen says to you,
'March with the word army
To fight against the great ants.'
Who after all are only great because
We are the obedient ants.

# IMPRISONED

Looking through a dirty window
Streaked with April rain,
I see a blurred vision of a
Girl in a white coat,
And?
In my head I feel a pain.

## ANTS AGAIN

Writing always writing
To shape a jungle of words
Madness to the ants
Who even if they read
Could not care less
But then
Perhaps Shakespeare
Was modern madness once.

## HOMOSEXUAL TEMPTATION
*(written during a storm)*

Lost between two living worlds
I stand on the brink of madness
Loving both for themselves
My heart thread bare of gladness
This lonely road which I tread
Fearing with each passing hour
Exposure with the condemnation
Of law and might of power
How could my dear love understand
This feeling for my true love
Unnatural to the law of man
Now weary I walk alone
With never a step to either side
All my hopes and faith
Is that God will be my guide.

## ATOMIC POEM THREE

I will love you still my dear
When all the world's on fire
And the birds no longer sing
The trees reduced to ashes
I will hold your fleshless hand
With my naked skeleton
And take you to the memories
By the stream where now we kiss
The fields that were green
Will be charred and black
But with burning feet
We will walk side by side
With our eyes to heaven
Heedless to the stench
Of the burning world
Two people in love
Together in atomic debris.

## RESPECTFUL REPLY TO DOM SILVESTER HOUÉDARD

Old fashion language with
Old fashion thoughts?
Surely this cannot be for a poet
Who does not think or live in your reality.
My world alone with God
Does not belong with the past
Or even with the future.
To die before my birth
That I do not live to die
So how is old fashion
When my words are now?
For you do not know tomorrow
Yet another pen in hand
It was still of yesterday
Fornicating in the courts
Persecuted at the reformation
And crying at the cross,
Did you not see me in the shadows
Always lonely and alone?
My love should well knows
That in every age
Where human bonds are present
I am there to suffer
With a spiritual knowledge
Of futile sex and bloody hate
Which in reality to you
Is the supreme of love in me.
God bless you my darling

I will always love you from afar
As I did in prehistoric days
And will in atomic debris.
Hand in hand with my poor friend
Who may have died in vain
Now he sees your living death
Who am I to judge?
My vocation into time
Is to feel for those who cannot
And suffer for those who will not.

## A QUESTION

Dear God where does it end
This day after day
And hum drum life?
The scene is so familiar now
I see it in my sleep
And hate it in my heart
The phone box on the corner
And the girl next door
Is it wrong to welcome death
With its change of scene
Or does it ever linger
Nostalgic memories of past loves
And then there is the current
How can we love
Is life just a farce dear Lord
A living motion picture
And am I just an actor
Dear God where does it end
This day after day
Will I ever love day after day?

## GHOST LIGHTS

I see your face in a certain place
A special corner of my room,
Where the sun first lights
After dark lonely nights
The shadow of fear becomes sweet you,
I awake with a start
Feeling in my heart that your vision
Is just a dream,
Then as it begins the hard rat race
I see again
Your ghostly face.

## CLARITY WITH DEATH

As now I'm dying
I see with clarity mistakes
No's that should have been yes
Decisions that were wrong
A girl I should have trusted
Advice I should have heard
But most of all I see
A bluish golden hue of perfect happiness
Lost in the shadows of everlasting hell.

# WATCHING

Whilst I was watching
My love my love
The days crept quietly by
Whilst I was watching
My true true love
I saw that first kiss not from me
Whilst I was watching
My sweet sweet love
The day you were married
My lost lost love
Your first dear child
Whilst I was watching
My life my hope my love
Then you passed by
Whilst I am dying
And I did not see you
My death my death.

## PLAIN OR CHEESE AND ONION?

Plain or cheese and onion?
The voice was hidden in an
Imperial tobacco mist,
Crowding people swam in
Intoxicated fumes
A small voice pleaded from
The neck of a driver's dirty
Brown overall,
'A mackeson until tomorrow missus',
Whilst she smiled with
Manufactured lips saying
'Tell yer mite ter keep 'is
'ands to 'isself.'
The juke box agreed yeah, yeah,
And a charming young lady
Quite drunk
Flopped out her tit right
Into the quiet man's face
Asking 'Wot yer fink of that?'
A man smiled at another across
The bar
And eyes made a hidden world
'Cross the reality of a London
Pub, on a Saturday night.

# FOG TELEGRAPHY

~1~
Hello there misty vision
Does fantasy always rule
Your path?
Do the trees that open up
To close you in
Belong to you or me?
Can I walk along the track
You walk above?
Could that chill night air
Float my heart
The way it does your body?
Are the dreams that fall from stars
Really tears you shed
For my poor mortal love?
Will the snowy slimness
Of your form
Ever bridge the gap to rest
In my arms?
Will your astral master ever
Allow your dear spirit
To stay awhile with mine
So that we might create
A mortal barrier between
good and evil?
Can love's powerful magic
Spite death's dark force
To tear my astral body
From all earthly ties?

~2~

May the great light master
Bless our task
OR
Am I just a pawn in a tremendous game?
Look now you must be real
For is that blood on my sheet
Where our lips bled farewell?
And is that not a crucifix
From some mystic plane
Hanging above my bed suspended in the air?
And is that not an evil eye
That watches from the corner?
Can we defy the clutching veins
Pouring pure human blood
So that all our roads are slippery
That we might slide into dark hell
To suffer eternal
Pains of love apart?
Who are you vision
To haunt my every
Waking hour?
Are you but
The dream of all men?

~3~
Is that rotting odour
Not the very devil?
Is not this clutching hand
Around my parched throat
Dark forces' strongest weapon?
As you fade dear vision
Could you not
Just blow a kiss
To dissolve this hopeless battle?
Or, my God
Are you part of them…?

# GOD IS A NIGGER

*New Poems by*

# William L. Stone

Citizen Publishing
Southend-on-Sea

Published 1964

Three shillings and sixpence

# MODERN POETRY

Modern poetry without rhythm
Or shame
Must seem to some or even most
A senseless jumble of words
But those who can read between
Each line
THE STORY
Which will show a tiny grain of sand
Among a beach of loves and hopes
Striving to find sympathy
(Just some who understand)
That a picture is not painted
Or a monument erected
For the appreciation of a living few
But rather for time who knows no death
Because the modern of today
Is the history of tomorrow.

# THE FOREIGNER

There they lay sleeping
The strangers
People of the day
Like a phantom I glide past
Their silent homes
Sailing with my ship on the canal
Our sadistic skipper blows hard
To shatter the holiness of night
Trees very dignified in anger
Seem to shush the rude intruder
Sitting on the capstan
Thinking as we pass each love's retreat
Who are the strangers
God's children of a foreign land
To realize with sadness
I am the foreigner
With a family
Who have never seen the atomium
Or the brazen little Brussels boy
Exploding nature in the city centre
I too have a family
And a silent home at night
But where is my morning wake
To the smell of egg and bacon love?
My mornings at sea are always foreign
And I am a lonely stranger.

# AGE
*Respectfully dedicated to Donald Geddes*

So when at last you've seen
The sun finally set,
And feel a coldness creeping in.
When you see the sweet young love
Of your youth
As a grey old lady.
When you see a child you knew
Leading armies into battle,
And every step is taken with
Painful laboured care,
As people help you across a
Busy road.
When you have only memories
Without dreams of tomorrow.
When everybody you meet
Reminds you of someone else,
And as you sleep alone at night
The pillow forms her breast
To lay your grey tired head.
When a smile no longer means
'I love you'
And your presence becomes a
Nuisance and a drag
When your wage
Is but a pension's pittance
And your socks someone's cast asides
As your eyes water in the slightest wind
When people call you dad instead of Jim

And gay young things
Mock your weary walk.
When flowers bring tears and signposts
Point to the past
When dogs bow their heads respectfully
As you pat them in passing
And God becomes more than just
A man in the shy
When angels seem to sing
In your deaf old ears,
And when at last you feel relieved
With a cold hand on your shoulder
Hearing a friendly voice say
'Come on Jim'
And your breast is full of sorrow
As you leave a sad old world
Be grateful to think
That tiny seed you planted
So many years ago
Is now a great tree bearing fruit
That will always be a part of you.

# FOR THE DEAD POETS AND OTHERS

We are the lost legion of life
The poets the painters and all creators
We who turn rejected love into things that last
Beyond the limits of time.
A monument to a scornful look or a friendly smile
From one adored by the passing symbol
Of God and man in a human shell.
That is why the pain is so deep
And my love too great for her
For it is the supreme of heaven
Dragged through the depth of hell
Caring as you scorn my love
For that is meant to be
If accepted me and I did not suffer
There would be no symbol of words
To carry my love to everlasting time.

# THE SHADOW

In my crofters home I see
A shadow on the wall
It does not move or talk
Like me it seems to be waiting.
A chill wind creeps into the night.
My eyes fix on the shadow
With grim expectancy.
Nothing happens the wind dies
Silence is with us again.
Then the stormy lightning
Stabs a sudden accusation
Into my barren crofters home
Revealing that the fault is mine.
The shadow splits in two
I cover my eyes with fear
Screaming pleading no
The rude intruder flees.
The shadow mends
Silence reigns again.
I stare at the shadow
To see a slow distortion.
A grinning bastard's head
The shadow is laughing at me.
Frenzied rage grips my body
I throw myself on the shadow
Pounding with solid blows.
Raw bone shows above my bleeding fist
My shirt wet with sweating fears
But I will destroy the shadow
As it has destroyed me.

## YEARS LATER...

Many years
She searched to find
His lonely crofters home
Her breast too full of love
For him to drink alone
To find but a dusty heap
Exposed by the noon sun
As a skeleton without a shadow

## MOVIE

History has been desecrated
Custer stands again
The gallant charge is led
Now it costs five bob
To see a man
Who should be dead.

# LAMENT OF A YOUNG POET

The knowledge was always their
Ignored but for time
Which makes fools of us all.
Lovers locked in each other's arms
Piecing desires of young virgins
Longing to be part of life's game.
I was born to create
So much more the appreciation
Of a girl in glowing purity
And false dignity of futile life.
Youth in its ignorance offers
Love with all abundance
But not for me whose life is words
Composed to order
Yet insults the crowing intellect
Of those who read and still love
The world.

## THOUGHTS IN A CHINESE RESTAURANT

I look at people
And see
Not people
But me!

## FOR DANIELLE

I will know her when we meet again
The familiar face that smiles in my dreams
We have been in love for ages
Although we cannot meet in this life
I know that somewhere in this world
Waits the golden girl of my dreams.
Her pony tail flies high and sends a message
In the never ending wind.
Danielle her eyes coloured in chocolate brown
And a satin skin to match awaiting my caress.
Of all the ventures we drift through
In our dreamy world
Like the time she held my hand
As we floated on a spongy cloud.
We kissed among the heavenly stars
The golden dust remained on our lips
A friendly star smiled at our embrace.
I long for the night to be with her again
To chase through endless fields of space
Her flapping pony tail screaming from ahead
I love you I love you
Then when at last I catch her
She willingly surrenders into my arms.
My darling you are but a dream
But I know that somewhere in another place
A golden girl with a pony tail is
Dreaming of me.

## FOR EILEEN

Deep in this complex nature
A tiny flame still burns
To send a little warmth
When my heart is cold.
The despair of lonely yearning
For the child who lit the fire
A Catholic girl with golden hair
I have not seen for years.
Perhaps the dolly in her pram
Is now a child in her arms
And if she is someone's mum
I will still think of her as
The little girl beside me
In a holy Catholic church.

# GOD IS A NIGGER

'GOD IS A NIGGER'
'GOD IS A NIGGER'
The chant rose to a crescendo
Whilst a small boy cried in defiance
**'God is white'**
They pushed and trampled until
His body turned to jelly and splattered
On the cobbled street.

The frenzied mob marched on still proclaiming
**'God is a nigger'**
Left in their bloody wake
The trampled mess stopped pulsating
And began to grow
A hideous grinning head appeared on the shoulders
That were once a Child's.
A tremendous voice announced behind the mob
**'God is here'**
They stopped afraid to turn
Silence cracked the air
No one moved not a breath of wind
Or a leaf dare to rustle.
Then from the midst of the crowd
Crawled a little girl with ebony skin
And topsy hair her teeth as white as virtue
Up to the monster she bravely swaggered
And looked to the height of his forbidding eyes
She simply quietly said
**'God is a nigger'**

## MARY JANE

I was with them this morning
(The train ants)
Kippered in a roaring tube
Unbearable sweaty bodies and
Hair spray fragrance.
My mind reverting to a forgotten past.
Suddenly a frightening realization
(I was thinking of you)
Those eyes, your eyes
Sweet deep brown
Telling lies as I stare into them.
My running past
To pause at last.
Mary Jane perhaps we'll never meet again
But this memory of my stormy way
Will leave a mark making you a part of me.
Soft beauty such as yours should never
Be exposed to a sad poet.
Mary Jane are now my living words
Described by this hand
That dares to transcribe your soul
To a world of dreams and hopes
In a fantasy land living dead.
If only we could have said hello
Before the battle,
Before the wounds,
Before the scars that never heal.
(Hello again Mary Jane in my dreams)
The battle is now fought and won.

Women had no place
Until among the crowd
I saw your face.
Mary Jane, Mary Jane
I say again
Sweet Mary Jane
To clutch a straw
This drowning man
Was washed ashore.
The beach is deep brown eyes
God blessed the meeting
A human devil forced the parting.
Please remember me quiet vision
I will still be dreaming
And reminiscing
Thinking that when we met
I somehow went to heaven.

## MESSAGE FOR A CHILD

Look from your study books
Dear child with youthful blessings
See through the school room window
The freely rolling clouds
On their endless journey around
A sad old tired world.
What secrets do they hold
Of lands they pass each day?
Seeing hungry dying people,
In the strange far away,
Bodies rotting from disease and war,
Babies that are never born,
Men fighting for dear life,
Others praying for deaths relief.
Stolen minutes of happiness,
With the world's forbidden lover,
Frenzied hours of sadness
For a child that's lost its mother,
So be glad to be beneath those
Rolling clouds,
In a warm and sturdy school,
But do not ignore my rule,
Which is remember always,
Those same rolling clouds
Also pass over you.

# UNTITLED POEMS

## POEM 1

Two hearts divided
Meeting on a level plain
Naked truth is undecided
To share a common pain
Two different lands apart
For each a foreign shore
Yet a bond feels each heart
Unbroken by some mystic law.
Two Gods, yet one the same
Classified by depth above
Finding error in a name
For whose God is the God of love?

## POEM 2

More colours to paint this scene.
Today a grey pigeon crashed into my car
Splattering it with the colour of our blood.
My car is island green
But she does not care either way
For what's one more dead pigeon?

## POEM 3

Now is the autumn of life.
The trees are casting
Leaves to the ground
Where they lay quite dormant
Lively coloured yet DEAD.
The sallow human child of God
Protests when the tree of life
Sheds him in creation's autumn.
Dust to dust for spring to see
Barren paths without a sign
Of the leaves that once were
ME.

*William L. Stone for
Revd. Fr. Brocard. 17/11/63*

## POEM 4

The world is a silent pool
Spirits of the dark abroad
Restless bodies leave their graves
Zombies obeying an evil lord.
Only those with astral sight
See this naked world
Where the forces of light
Caught by the setting sun are held.
An ageless march where time is still
Rotting flesh preserved to warn
What man never knew.
Crushed pulp of human bone

Is now waiting for me
All night I hear them calling
A restless soul is crying
My lost love I am going.

## POEM 5

I don't suppose that now
You like to read my poems
Anymore
I don't suppose you care
If I am no more.
But then I don't suppose I care
If you read my poems anymore
Because what I feel for you words
Won't make you feel that way for me.

## POEM 6

The value of human position
Can be compared to taking a
Drop of water and pouring it
Over the peak of a mountain,
Then waiting at the bottom
To catch the remains.

## BIZARRE THOUGHTS

The parting of today
Is the meeting of tomorrow

If all the tiny stars
Were the dreams of man,
Would they not be wasted
In the emptiness of space.
For is not space only full
Of stars,
And are not the lives of men,
Only full of deams

To commit suicide is like
Blowing out a candle
In the middle of a
Summer's day

There are two forces
In the astral life,
Dark and light,
Men are neither.

Today's knowledge
Is tomorrow's ignorance

God is not really
rocks and things,
he is that which
casts the lives of

men, as men cast
the laying rocks

Pains in the head international
By invitation

POLAND pistol point truths

For our absent friend,
A verse
It is not the first,
And it's not the last

Male prostitution
Grimm's 'Fairy' tales

Smiles that intrude
Our misery

Condescending sunshine
Oozing
With charity

Stretching memories of perished elastic.

Pickled geisha girls
In frosted glass jars

# TWO CONCRETE POEMS

## *Dedication*

My friend dom Silvester Houe'dard was a mentor and influence in the world of poetry. This addition to *Forty Odd Years On* is in recognition of DSH.

Concrete Poem 1 'The Paper Boy' was written in the 60s and originally included in my collection *God Is A Nigger*. Concrete Poem 2 reflects my vision of concrete poetry today.

*Concrete poetry* is poetry in which the typographical arrangement of words is as important in conveying the intended effect as the conventional elements of the poem, such as meaning of words, rhythm, rhyme and so on. It is sometimes referred to as *visual poetry*, a term that has evolved to have distinct meaning of its own, because the words themselves form a picture.

The term was coined in the 1950s, and in 1956 an international exhibition of concrete poetry was shown in São Paulo, Brazil, inspired by the work of Carlos Drummond de Andrade

## Concrete Poem I

## THE PAPER BOY

**hum hum dng dng dng hum hum
dng dng hum dng dng hum dng
dng hum dng dng hum dng dng
dng hum dng hum hum dng
hum hum hum hum hum hum**

**hummmmmmmmmmdngggggg**

## Concrete Poem 2
# FAREWELL DEPARTED WIFE AND FRIENDS

SHERRY

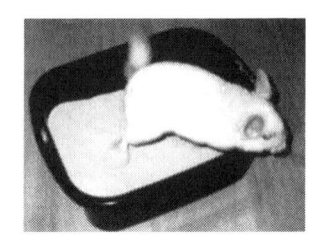

CID

GWEN, BONNIE & CLYDE

JINTA AND JANTA

MOOJA, REX & SHEBA

LUKE AND LUCY

# LEBANON INSPIRED POEMS

*by Yasmin Hussein*

# THE BEAUTY OF LEBANON

The sight of the sun sitting on the mountain tops,
Reflecting lights of gold, orange and red,
Telling us to be off to bed.

But the stars! Oh the stars!
How they glimmer at night.
Millions of stars so beautiful, so bright.
With a full moon, casting the shadows delivering its
Silver lights.
It truly is a wonderful sight.

But best of all, the sounds of nature;
The gentle breeze through the trees,
Making the leaves quiver.
The crickets playing the tune of love and peace.
The night animals to roam as they please.
How could a person sleep
When there is such beauty to see?

*Yasmin Hussein*

# SECRETS

These words come as a whisper
With hardly a sound,
These words could be important
So listen to me now,
These words go to you
But nobody else,
These words are never to be told, heard, or known
These words should never be found.
Kept between you and me,
And doesn't exist against the crowd
These words are secrets
And should never be told out loud.

*Yasmin Hussein, aged 12*

## THE VOICE

'You're fat'
'You're ugly'
'You're worthless'
Is what people said
'Everyone's better off without me'
Said the voice inside her head
Every day it got worse,
Too much for her to bear
She wanted to tell her mother but
'Why would she care?'
Her only friend was the voice
That told her what to do
It said she should stop eating and to cut herself too.
Oh what a shame it was when she finally broke down
She couldn't take it anymore
If only her mother had come home sooner
She would have saved her life
She found her in a puddle of blood
And next to her a knife.

*Yasmin Hussein, aged 13*

## THE SANDMAN

Oh little boy!
Why are you still awake?
Don't worry my child,
I am here to chase your nightmares away.
I will sprinkle my sand over your eyes,
To bring you sweet dreams and a pleasant night.
Softly and slowly you close them tight,
Sleep until the morning light.

*Yasmin Hussein, aged 14*

## HOME SWEET HOME

Down the street and around a corner,
There I meet a lawful soldier,
Holding his gun with a mocking glance
As I silently pass.

Another turn and down the alley way
Through the crowded space.
There was a wider lane,
Much less dark and much less narrow,
But it was only meant for the new people who had come,
If I was to walk there, my life would surely be done!

I walk faster as I approach a group of them,
I walk pass them as they laugh and sneer
When they point at me, I cower in fear.
I walk into the mosque and pray

Praying for peace, praying for a better day.
A day where we can all walk down the same lane,
A day where we are all the same,
Where home feels like home,
When our suffering will be known,
After all, their guns hurt more than our stones.

*Yasmin Hussein, aged 15*

## THE MEANING OF LIFE

The lotus pod germinates
In the shallowest part of the waters,
Born in darkness.
Reaching for the warmth of the sunlight,
Pushing its way through the murky water.
Growing, growing.
Its hand reaches the surface,
Opening to welcome the summer light,
Blooming in all the prettiest of colours.
Free from the shadows from hence it came,
With the beauty of a lioness.
Despite conditions endured progressed.

*Yasmin Hussein, aged 16*

## LIKE A STONE

Like a stone,
I stood my ground,
Unmoved by the wind and rain.
My principles stand strong,
Embedded in my brain.
You may step on me all you want,
But I will show no pain,
Because like a stone,
I shall not break.
Like a stone,
I remain.

## THE TRAIN RIDE

I looked out of the window,
Up at the sky to pray;
I had no idea what to say.
'Forgive me for rejecting you
But everything I love is moving further away.
I beg you please, please let me stay.'
I pleaded for ages,
But no answer came.
The train finally stopped
And I knew my life would never be the same.

# LEBANON INSPIRED POEMS

## *by Bill Stone*

# THOUGHTS ON CHRISTMAS DAY

There is a wind passing by
On this Christmas day
It's free and travelling high
With a message for you to say
'Granddad hopes you are safe
With memories remaining of me
When no longer of the human race
In the knowledge of eternity'
You chose to run and think free
From what? and to a place called where?
Will at times be a wild and stormy sea
I know this because I have been there
When life gets tough and the going rough
Put your thoughts into words and sentences
Show that your decisions are of mighty stuff
And your book of life will break down fences
Most of all my Grandchild at times pause,
Remember your family love you unconditionally
No matter what you judge as the reason, the cause?
The for your chosen sojourn
Will in time be revealed.

*Christmas Day, 2016*

# UNTITLED LEBANON POEMS

**~1~**
Stream I do not know your name
Rushing with intent
Playing some dark game
Carrying nature's debris like a vent.
People react insanely in your presence
Whilst bathing in your wetness
As if seeking lost in life an essence
Mocking reality as a madness.
My conveyance to Lebanon
In an airborne coffin
Grabbing body and soul up and away
My memories still contained within.
Although I reject this grave like intrusion
I will return to a chosen recluse
Now repairing my life's blown fuse
With Lebanon's regenerated infusion.
Eventually I intend a spectacular return
Self-winged powered by MEA
Without a burden of negative concerns
An inspired future flowers.
Rejuvenated I take a new stance
Against accepting corruption
And all other political nonsense
Purveyors with feel my eruption.
My future will reflect from the past
Without pity for those with no life
My space wider at last
Sensing a bond with my departed wife.

~2~
There the sadness of sadness
The equaliser in continuous life
Necessary to balance insanity
Or alternative to a dormant host.
Then when contemptuous dagger thrust
Ripping the souls from natures creations
Our conscience becomes a blinkered coward
Remaining oblivious in a state of denial.
Who dares to accuse the bad man?
What guilt appoints a bad man?
For the bad man is in us all
The epitome? we are all the bad man.
Farewell, farewell again old Lebanon
Both a land of ugly deeds and beauty
There can be no other sane comparison
To this coexistence in a blinkered crucible.

~3~
No I'm looking thru the widows of my closing life
Frustrated because my vision is not clear
The answers I desire are surely there
But
Unrecognisable faces are not those I seek
Poses the question 'Am I no longer alive,
Or just a figment of imagination?'

~4~
A face of a host who is no more
Is impregnated on this rock that I hold
The past remains as now
Matter reconstructed a moment of time

With my touch now is superseded
Flowing on a tributary called eternity
Towards a sanctuary of meaning
Within a permanent estate.

## THOUGHTS

I don't stroll down memory lane
And I don't even think about you.
I don't think about tomorrow
And I don't care about the world.
Although.
I do care about a snail crushed from spite.
I do care about cattle being slaughtered.
I do care about culling nature with a concrete jungle,
I do care about a seagull's broken wing.
Then
Then I see many other birds in flight.
With a vision of who is waiting for me.
Thus I will join life's migrating flight
Now
Now I will follow that path to destiny
To hopefully find my lost soulmates.
I will re-join my sojourn to a destiny
That is free and far beyond human darkness.

## SICK HUMOUR?

Don't cry my little man.
Daddy will buy you a gun
Then you can shoot mummy
Then we can both have fun.

## A BEGGAR'S DOG

The others, the people, friends, that I knew
All past away and gone to 'GOD?'
A myth than many believe in hope
Not to the hell of being a beggar's dog

At least I have freedom to live my way
Not condemned to being a prop without a choice
To extort money for a dysfunctional human
As the fate of a beggar's dog without a voice

The beggars claim to be destitute and homeless
Then condemn an innocent dog to the same fate
Soliciting cash from compassionate naive people
Funding habit and lifestyle they would really hate

## I SAW A SAD DOG!

I saw a sad dog today
Tied up by Sainsbury's
Waiting
Just waiting
I spoke to a sad dog today
Its ears slightly acknowledged
Whilst waiting
Still waiting

## SLOW IS THE SNAIL

Slow is the snail and slower the slug
Fast is a sparrow faster a gull
Slowly time passes for the young
To the old a grave is already dug.

Tomorrow never comes is proven wrong
When all you have is yesterdays
It's a lie to say that love never dies
For where is life and love now she is gone?

Snails, slugs, sparrow and gull remain
Cats, dogs, wildlife co-exist in time
Though none for me to waste or wait
For I will never see her again.

If after death there are choices
It's a creature of nature I want to be
Without human despicable creations
Giving deceptive promises from a myriad of voices.

# MAYBE?

So I talk to animals, trees, walls
And other innate
Objects
Including you
Boredom maybe?
But when they reply
It's time to question
Why?
The impossible voices chattering
An answer to mortality
Fear?
So now there's the depression of a selfish world
Including you politicians and clerics
Maybe
The flaw of this existence is the creation
Of an invented God
To avoid the conclusion
Reality is Supernature.

## AN ANATOMY OF IDIOSYNCRASIES

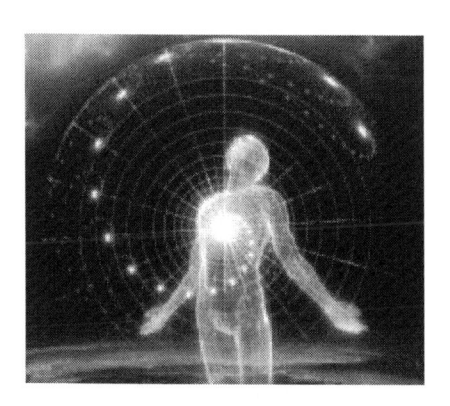

Searching and seeing but is it now too late
Are these mocking images sadly just surreal
Leaving me determined to be alone with fate
And consciousness a cruel spinning wheel?
All animal companions gave me comfort
Most human actions resulted in deep despair
From the malicious destruction that they sort
Causing other life to be intolerable and unfair.
In desperation I grasp a straw of fading memory
Striving hopelessly to reincarnate some lost life
A self-failing mission determination to go awry
Fuelled with the guilt of rejecting my dead wife.
Onward or outward
In all quantum space and directions
An uncontrollable reminiscence
Of a spirit turned projectile
Without even comfort from freedom
Of embodied imperfections
Or even a latent claim of peace
That it was all worthwhile.

*Those that now tread in the steps*
*Following my demise*
*Witness the evidence of matter*
*In all that physically exists*
*The nucleus of a rock*
*May still contain atoms of my eyes*
*Thus in the crucible of structures*
*I will eternally persist.*

# THE NOT SO GRIM REAPER

*A One-Act Play*

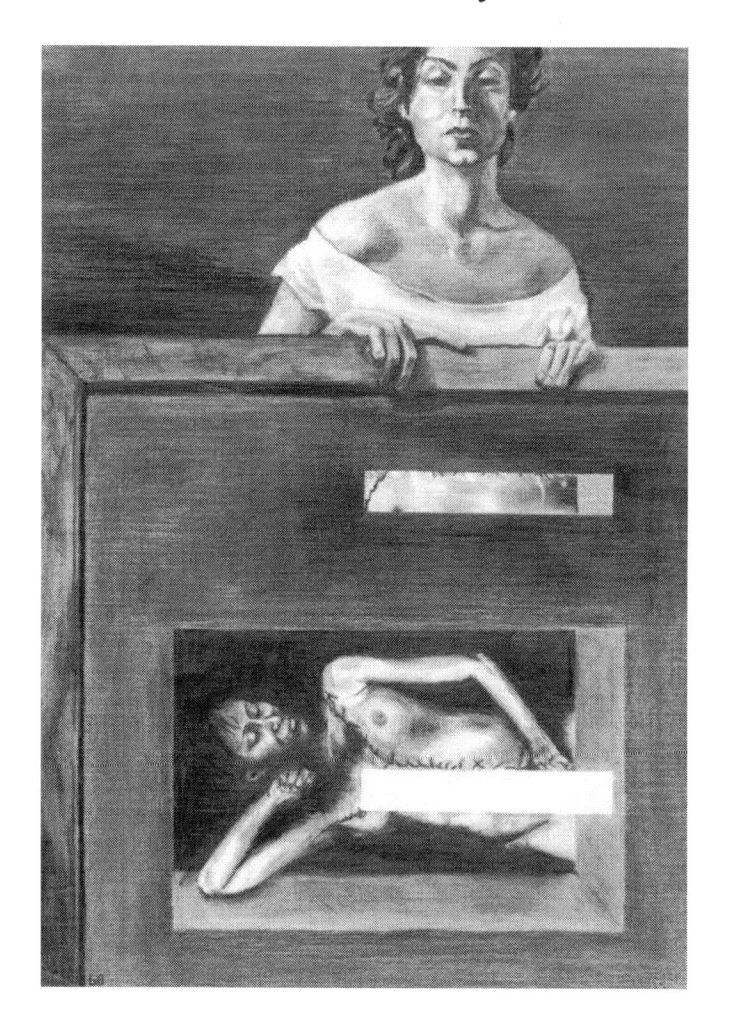

# The Not So Grim Reaper

NARRATOR: Whilst drifting aimlessly on the wing of a dream Sam flew into a vortex of air. The swirling mass dragged him down towards a hospital below. He hit the building but passed through the structure. He stopped above a scene in an operating theatre. He recognised the patient as himself and heard the surgeon say 'All done'.
(*Pause*)
NARRATOR: Sam is sleeping. The hospital ward is uncannily quiet. A female voice calls to him.
VOICE: Sam, Sam.
SAM: (*Drowsily awakening*) Y, yes?
VOICE: It's me Alika. How are you today dear?
SAM: I don't know anyone called Alika.
ALIKA: So you don't know love then?
SAM: (*Wide awake*) Pardon? I don't understand.
ALIKA: My name is Alika; it's Muslim meaning love.
SAM: Oh, very nice. Are you a nurse? I don't remember seeing you before.
ALIKA: No I am a visitor. You are quite ill so probably you do not realise that I am always here.
SAM: Always?
ALIKA: (*Smiling*) Shall we say always metaphorically speaking because isn't love always there if you look for it?
SAM: (*Attempting humour*) I can't speak metaphoric but I do know 'salam halakum' and 'Inshalla'. That's Muslim, isn't it?

133

| | |
|---|---|
| ALIKA: | Of course. So you still have Beirut in your mind? |
| SAM: | How do you know I was in Beirut? |
| ALIKA: | Love is in Beirut also Sam. Did you not see me there? |
| SAM: | (*Feeling spooked*) Yes. (*Sadly whimsical*) Oh yes I met love there but her name was not Alika. |
| ALIKA: | Widad? That is also an Arabian name meaning love. |
| SAM: | How do you know about Widad? |
| ALIKA: | Maybe I can read your mind and see the hurt lying there? |
| SAM: | I'll never forget her. (*Stares intently at Alika.*) You bear a striking resemblance to her. |
| ALIKA: | Look again Sam. Maybe the resemblance was in your mind? |
| SAM: | (*Confused as he looks again at her.*) Oh my God! |
| ALIKA: | Her name meant 'Born again'. |
| SAM: | Am I dreaming? I now see a resemblance to Renee in you. |
| ALIKA: | When you look at love it takes on many forms. It's very true 'Beauty is in the eyes of the beholder.' |
| SAM: | I miss them both. They died so young and so tragically. Renee, my wife, was only twenty-eight and I held her as she passed away from cancer. Widad was even younger she also died in my arms from wounds received during an Israeli invasion into Lebanon. Her last words to me were: 'Sam why do these people want to kill me? I am young and help my dad look after the family since my mom died |

|  |  |
|---|---|
| | and I work hard at my office to bring money home. I am a good Muslim and I don't hurt or hate anybody. Why Sam? Why? I want to live and marry and have children like my Mom.' Then she died with tears flowing from her eyes. |
| ALIKA: | (*Weeping*) I know Sam. I know. Human nature at times becomes the personification of utter evil. Power, greed and self gratification replace the need to love. |
| | *The ward comes alive as if suddenly switched on.* |
| PATIENT 1: | (*Calling loudly*) Nurse, nurse I need a bottle quickly I am peeing myself. |
| PATIENT 2: | (*Attempting to shout over Patient 1*) Nurse, nurse, *nurse!* Henry is out of bed again and taking my things. |
| HENRY: | (*Shouting*) they are *my* things, liar. You are all liars and the nurses are all liars. They are drugging me and keeping me against my will. They are all employed by Hitler to use us as human guinea pigs. (*Two nurses appear on the scene as Henry runs out of the ward screaming.*) Bastards! Bastards! Bastards! (*The nurses chase after him.*) |
| SAM: | It's always like this. There are several patients with psychological problems who at one time would have been placed in a psychiatric ward, but now they lump everyone in together. The nurses are kept busy keeping them in bed and other patients get neglected. |
| | *Alika does not comment and he turns towards her to see why. She is not there.* |

|  |  |
|---|---|
| | *Sam stares at the place she stood until dropping back to sleep.* |
| NURSE: | Sam, Sam. It's time for your injection. *Opens his eyes and recognises the nurse.* |
| SAM: | OK. Has Alika gone? |
| NURSE: | Alika? |
| SAM: | The visitor who came to see me? |
| NURSE: | You have been dreaming, Sam. Visiting is not until four o'clock. It's only one-thirty. |
| SAM: | But *(pauses)* OK. *Nurse prepares the injection and is about to administer it when Henry charges by.* |
| HENRY: | *(Shouting)* Bastards! The British army will rescue us and you will all be shot for crimes against humanity. Evil bastards! |
| NURSE: | *(Panicking)* Oh my God! *She gives chase with the syringe still in her hand.* |
| PATIENT 1: | *(Shouting)* Oh no! Toby is out of bed now! |
| TOBY: | *(Following the nurse chasing Henry and calls after them)* All right, all right, Henry. I am coming. |
| PATIENT 1: | It's a mad house not a hospital! |
| SAM: | What's going to happen to my injection? |
| PATIENT 2: | I hope she sticks it right up Henry's arse. |
| PATIENT 1: | *(Maliciously)* Be better up the eye of his dick. |
| SAM: | Did you see that Asian-looking lady who visited me? |
| PATIENT 1: | No but I saw you talking to the bottom of your bed earlier? |
| PATIENT 2: | Yea, so did I. Perhaps you're going senile like Henry and Toby? |
| SAM: | Probably. I came in here having had bowel cancer successfully removed but |

the chemotherapy made me very ill. Now I have all sorts wrong with me, so yes I am probably senile as well. If Alika was imagination, that's the Asian girl I saw, senility isn't so bad because she was absolutely beautiful.

PATIENT 1: Wow! I want some of what you are on and with a bit of Viagra would have a fantastic time with her.

PATIENT 2: Me too. It's been so long now that I am beginning to fancy that male nurse that minces around the ward.

PATIENT 1: (*Defensively*) Don't knock it. He's the best nurse on this ward.

SAM: Yes he gets his priorities right. He would not have run after Henry with my injection.

PATIENT 2: Mind you, I reckon he gets regular injections but not administered by a syringe?

SAM: For Christ's sake, man. Have you no respect?

PATIENT2: Sorry. I was at sea too long and forget that shore side humour is very different from mine.

PATIENT1: What boats were you on?

PATIENT2: None but lifeboats because its ships that we sailed on not boats. Boats are what little boys play with in the bath.

PATIENT 1: I didn't play with boats in my bath.

PATIENT 2: (*Sarcastically*) No, we know what you played with in your bath (winks at Sam) *Nurse returns with Henry holding her hand. The other hand still contains Sam's injection. Toby follows behind marching like a rear guard. The day passes and*

|  |  |
|---|---|
|  | *visiting time arrives. Sam scrutinises the entries hoping Alika would come.* |
| SAM: | *(Thinking aloud)* She's not coming. |
| HENRY: | *(Still shouting)* They have gassed her! |
| SAM: | Shut up, Henry. |
| PATIENT 1: | Yea shut up, Henry. I wish they would gas you! |
| HENRY: | Fascist pig. Your turn will come mate. Don't say I didn't warn you. Escape if you can. I am in charge of the escape committee but keep getting caught and brought back. But if you manage to get out tell the allies to bomb this concentration camp. Even if they kill us all! It's better dead than being tortured here. |
| SAM: | Please shut up, Henry. |
| HENRY: | Collaborator! |
| PATIENT 2: | Have you been in the army, Henry? |
| HENRY: | Don't know. |
| PATIENT 2: | How old are you, Henry? I heard a nurse say you are 92? |
| HENRY: | Don't know. |
| PATIENT 2: | Don't know a lot, do you? |
| HENRY: | Pig! |
|  | *Sam dozes off and awakes later to find the visitors have left with the exception of a lady talking to Henry.* |
| SAM: | *(Calls out)* Alika? |
|  | *The visitor at Henry's bed turns toward him then returns her attention to the conversation she is having with Henry.* |
| SAM: | *(Repeating)* Alika. |
|  | *She ignores him.* |

## Still a Poet at 80? 139

PATIENT 1: Old Henry doesn't sound too good. He is muttering away to himself and sounds distressed?
SAM: Alika is talking to him.
PATIENT 1: What? You losing it completely, mate? He's talking to himself.
SAM: But... (*Gives up trying to respond.*)
PATIENT 1: He's gone silent. Something is not right.
PATIENT 2: Call the nurse I don't think he is breathing.
NURSE: (*Pulls the curtains around Henry's bed.*) Oh dear.
PATIENT 2: (*Calls*) Is he dead?
AUTHORITIVE VOICE: Shush, be quiet.
PATIENT 2: Bollocks:

**Several days later**
    *Sam has been quite ill and confused he awakes staring at the empty bed formerly occupied by Henry.*
ALIKA: He died, Sam.
SAM: Where did you come from? I did not see you enter the ward. What time is it?
ALIKA: It's...
PATIENT 1: Welcome back, Sam. Did you know that Henry managed to escape?
SAM: Escape?
PATIENT 1: Yea, he died.
SAM: This is Alika. She was with Henry when he died.
PATIENT 1: (*Puzzled*) Who is Alika? Sorry to spoil your dreams mate but there is nobody there. Don't worry, old chap. I often see people who are not there. Wishful thinking eh?

| | |
|---|---|
| SAM: | (*Feeling foolish and changes the subject*) I feel sorry for his daughter. She was the only visitor he had. |
| PATIENT 1: | I don't. She was a selfish cow. On the day before he died I heard her trying to persuade him to go into a nursing home. 'For your own good, Dad,' she said. I know Henry was not short of a bob or two and had a large detached house. That's what the bitch was after! |
| SAM: | Oh? |
| PATIENT 1: | Yea oh! |
| | *Toby gets out of bed and starts walking out of the ward* |
| TOBY: | They have gassed Henry. |
| PATIENT 1: | No they haven't. He died. Where do you think you are going? |
| TOBY: | Died, why? I was going to tell the authorities what these people are doing to us. |
| PATIENT 1: | Tell them that the staff can't do their jobs properly because they spend so much time chasing nutters like you and Henry. |
| TOBY: | Fuck off. |
| PATIENT 1: | Nutter! |
| SAM: | Leave him alone. He's harmless. |
| PATIENT1: | (*Sarcastically*) I wish he were legless. That would stop him getting out of bed needlessly and causing strife for the nurses. |
| | *The image of Alika is no longer visible. Sam turns his attention towards Henry's empty bed.* |
| SAM: | (*Addressing the mental image of Alika.*) Why were you there when he died? |

ALIKA'S VOICE: I told you, Sam, love is everywhere and has a place at death, but, sadly, many cannot recognise it.
SAM: I can't see you?
ALIKA: No, but you can feel and hear me. Sadly so many people cannot see, hear or feel me either.
SAM: Very true. There are many aspects of love though. Like the love of a friend without the intimacy of passion or the love of animals, children and God?
ALIKA: You do not believe in God, Sam.
SAM: No, but I do believe in those that sincerely believe in God. Like Widad, she was always praying for me to become a Muslim. I do not believe, however, in the abuse of the followers of a religion by their supposed mentors. However, I do believe in the possibility of life after death. I feel that in whatever way this might bear on the human condition, most of us are not necessarily capable of comprehending such transcendental states in our daily lives. My personal view is that human life is far removed from that of the spiritual, and is generally flawed and corrupt. Genuinely religious people are 'beautiful' souls. However, there are also those who masquerade as religious, or use religion for their own ends, especially those misguided, self-centred and quite possibly evil people who have the power and authority, and use the vehicle of faith to pursue inhuman activities.
ALIKA: (*Pensive*) Oh?

SAM: (*Eager to continue*) I think the God that people believe in is a personal manufactured excuse to justify their own inadequacies. It is also a sense of having security, possibly in prayer to combat the insecurity of life. That God is also a personal image – for instance, does a black child visualise God as the white man of Jesus? I think not. I once heard a story that illustrated the illusion. (*His voice becomes audible to the other patients*) God sent a senior angel to travel Earth spreading the message. After visiting many of the world's capital cities, the Angel arrived in London. Whilst flying low and enjoying the scene the Angel collided with a double-decker bus. One of his wings was damaged and the Angel was rushed to Saint Thomas Hospital. Under the care of a very skilled surgeon the wing was successfully repaired. On the day of discharge from the hospital, the Angel asked to see the surgeon and said to him, 'You are a wonderful person and discharge God's creation of mankind in the way of his intention. I would like to reward you by way of a thank you from God and myself. Is there anything that you wish for?' The surgeon with courtesy replied 'No thank you, I have my work and a good life and cannot think of anything that would improve it.' The Angel looked disappointed, causing the surgeon to relent. 'There is something. Like all people I am curious about the nature of God. Can you tell me about

|  |  |
|---|---|
|  | him?' The Angel thought for a moment and then said, 'That is the most guarded secret in Heaven. But God agrees that I can tell you because he trusts you not to reveal the truth. And the truth is she's Black!' |
| ALIKA: | Point taken, Sam. |
| SAM: | You sound angry? |
|  | *Alika does not reply.* |
| PATIENT 1: | That's fantastic. Never heard anyone put it better. (*Sarcastically*) Were you telling it to me or that invisible girlfriend of yours? Got any more religious jokes? |
| SAM: | (*Humouring him*) Well, there is the story about the man who became a monk. |
| PATIENT 1: | Please tell me. |
| PATIENT 2: | Blasphemous bastard! You will rot in hell. |
| PATIENT 1: | Ignore him. He's another mad bible basher. |
| SAM: | Well, this man entered a closed order of monks that take a vow of silence. He had an audience with the Abbot and was told, 'Every five years the brothers come to me and say two well chosen words so I look forward to your first uttering.' The five years soon passed and the man, now a monk, appeared before the Abbot. 'I have been looking forward to this, Brother. What have you chosen to say?' The monk bowed before his mentor and said, 'Soup's cold.' The Abbot clapped gleefully. 'How constructive. What a positive comment. I look forward to seeing you again in five years for your next words.' It was now the tenth year of the |

man's monastic life and he was before the abbot again. 'I am so pleased to see you again, Brother, and what have you to say this time?' 'Soup's cold,' repeated the monk. The Abbot clapped and said, 'I am so happy that you are still being observant and positive. I look forward to the next time.' Well, the fifteenth year came and the monk went before the Abbot who made the usual invitation to speak. The monk said, 'I'm leaving.' The Abbot replied 'Thank God for that because you have done nothing but moan for the past fifteen years.'

*The rattle of the food trolley announces the arrival of the Filipino catering assistant. Her English is limited. This causes communication problems with the patients.*

CATERING ASSISTANT: (*Calls out*) Foody, foody.
PATIENT 1: Crappy, crappy.
CAT. ASS.: (*Takes Patient 1 seriously.*) Sorry, crappy, crappy? (*Looks at patient's name tag and delivers his pre-ordered meal.*) Nice crappy foody for you, meester.
PATIENT 1: (*Inspecting the plate*) As usual this is not what I ordered!
CAT. ASS.: Yes very nice. Thank you, meester.
PATIENT 1: *No! No! No!* Not very nice. It's not mine. You shouldn't be allowed to serve the food if you can't speak English.
CAT. ASS.: Yes English, thank you.
SAM: What is it?
PATIENT 1: It's roast beef and I ordered chicken.
SAM: I've got chicken and ordered beef; get her to swap them.

| | |
|---|---|
| PATIENT1: | How? She won't understand? (*Calls to the catering assistant, cruelly mimicking her with deliberate exaggeration.*) Swappy mine with Meester Sam. |
| CAT. ASS.: | (*Sensing the ridicule*) No have not got. Thank you. |
| TOBY: | (*Gets out of bed and swaps the lunches over.*) It's probably all dog meat anyway or maybe left over's from the gas chambers. Hey perhaps we are eating old Henry? |
| CAT. ASS.: | Dog not can come in hospital. And not to speak bad about Meester Henry please. |
| TOBY: | OK, I'll just do your job for you and shut up. Eh? |
| CAT. ASS.: | OK. Thank you. (*She smiles.*) |
| | *Nurse arrives carrying a syringe with an injection for Sam.* |
| NURSE: | A little prick for you, Sam. |
| PATIENT 1: | Wow. That sounds exciting. |
| SAM: | Are you actually going to inject me or chase somebody with it? |
| NURSE: | Sarcasm is the lowest form of wit, Sam. |
| TOBY: | I bet Sam would like to give you a little prick, nurse. |
| NURSE: | He should be so lucky. |
| | *Catering assistant leaving the ward, overhears the conversation, and laughs.* |
| CAT. ASS.: | Ha! Mister Sam gotta little pricky, eh? |
| PATIENT 1: | She understood that all right. |
| | *Sam's eyes drooped and he became drowsy his head dropped into a nodding position.* |
| ALIKA: | How are you, dear? |
| SAM: | (*Startled on hearing her voice.*) Alika? |
| ALIKA: | Was you expecting someone else? |

| | |
|---|---|
| SAM: | I was not expecting anyone, although I am always hoping that you are here. |
| ALIKA: | I've always been here, Sam, and always will be. |
| SAM: | I love you. |
| ALIKA: | I know and I love you. |
| SAM: | Until death us do part? |
| ALIKA: | Not beyond that, dear? |
| SAM: | But I do not understand what is happening. I am in hospital and know that I have been very ill. Yet I cannot remember before being here. Are we in a relationship? |
| ALIKA: | (*Avoiding the question.*) We love each other Sam, and when this hospital period is over everything will be clear to you. We will be happy together. |
| SAM: | Why do I feel so disorientated? It feels as if I have I have been in a coma for a long time and have awakened to a different world. People I knew are no longer about, and there is an alien culture all around me. Then there is you, although I know that I love you, but you are also the same but different. When you were talking to Henry the night he died I was jealous and angry. It was a possessive emotion: you are my friend and also my love and I did not want to share you. |
| ALIKA: | That's always been the problem with love, Sam. Spiritual love is unconditional and develops in another place. But physical love is born out of a destructive element, In some men the objective of love is to make the target a trophy desired by other men but unobtainable because it |

|  |  |
|---|---|
|  | is owned by the lover. Spiritual love once created remains forever dedicated to the soulmate for which it is meant. The challenges of 'trophy' love separate the souls and the physical is often transferred to a new partner. The spiritual soulmate love remains lost in eternity until reunited. |
| SAM: | That's why people seem to look for similar characteristics of their first love in the ones that follow. |
| ALIKA: | Exactly. |
| SAM: | The foundation of our love, Alika, is that unconditional element that you spoke of. If for some reason we lost sight of each other for a long time on reunification we would continue as if the break had not happened? |
| ALIKA: | That is what is happening now, dear. In the confusion caused by illness you are seeking to retrogress to a time when we were happy in our relationship of unconditional love. |
| SAM: | Yes, I understand. It's like living in parallel worlds where everything that we have ever done we are still doing coexistent with the present. The bodies are different, but the spirits remain constant? |
| ALIKA: | Come with me Sam. (*Holds out a hand to help him out of bed.*) Sam and Alika leave the ward hand in hand. |
| NURSE: | (*Arrives with an injection for Sam.*) Oh dear, he's gone. |
| TOBY: | Gone where? |

| | |
|---|---|
| PATIENT 1: | (*Replies*) DEAD!<br>(*The lights fade and the patients sleep. During the night Toby awakes and sees ALIKA standing at his bedside*) |
| ALIKA: | Hello Toby, do you remember me? |
| TOBY: | You look like Mavis but she died five years ago? |
| ALIKA: | You have been very ill, Toby, but you do remember love. |
| TOBY: | Yes I have never forgotten you 'Mavis'? |
| ALIKA: | I've never been far away, darling. Just waiting and watching as you grew older and suffered the loneliness of absent love but I have come to tell you that love is eternal, Toby. |
| TOBY: | Will we be young and together again, Mavis? |
| ALIKA: | True love is not physical, Toby. It is spiritual. The spirit is unbound on death to become complete in eternity. |
| TOBY: | That's a wonderful thought. (*She holds her hand towards Toby.*) |
| ALIKA: | Come dear, it's time to go.<br>(A *nurse discovers that Toby is dead and summons a colleague.*) |
| NURSE: | Thee deaths this week. It's astounding. |
| PATIENT 1: | It's that woman! |
| NURSE: | What woman? |
| PATIENT 1: | I'm saying no more. Don't want her visiting me. |
| NARRATOR: | No chance mate. You have never known love. (*Pauses then begins to recite*)<br>  So finally the sun has set<br>    Your life is at its end.<br>  The voice that you hear<br>  The hand that beckons |

>           Tell you that she is here.
>           Rise from your deathbed
>             To follow that dove
>           Fly with her to eternity
>           To be reunited with your love.
>           (*30 seconds pause*)

ALL:        To be reunited with your love.

**CURTAIN**

# THAT'S ALL NOW FOLKS

*And finally by my grandson, CLINTON SMITH, a Hells Angel biker who wrote this poem for his wife just before his death at 31 years of age.*

'That's all now folks,
It's over now,
I've had my time
If I had it again,
I would do the same.
All the fights,
And all the love bites,
All the times I've fallen down drunk,
And the times I've smoked skunk,
Don't cry for me, he said,
Not just because I am dead.
If life after death is true,
I will be there enjoying myself,
Smoking a joint while I wait for you.
If it's only bullshit,
Then I won't know,
Nor will you until it's time for you to go.
Don't cry for what I have not got,
In life I had more than most,
Don't cry for me because I am dead,
Go out and get pissed instead,
You have not lived until you have died,
I know, I tried!
Ps. Roach in pocket

*Clinton Smith, 1964–96*

# APPENDIX

A British Airways *Evening Standard* newspaper promotion

Win a plane for 50 people to Edinburgh
Celebrating 10 years at London City Airport
Monday, 29 April 2013, 09:29

In 2003, British Airways began flying from London City Airport and changed the face of business and pleasure travel for Londoners. To celebrate the ten year landmark, over the past six weeks we have been giving readers the chance to win a short break to amazing destinations.

In this final week, you could win flights on a private BA plan to Edinburgh – for you and up to 49 friends – from London City Airport.

The prize also includes accommodation at the Sheraton Grand Hotel & Spa for one night, and an Edinburgh Pass, granting free entry to various attractions.

Edinburgh is a cultural haven and a creative paradise. Show us your creativity by sending us a limerick or poem telling us why you should win the plane.

**Terms & Conditions:**

Promotion closes at 23:59 on 6 May 2013. There is one prize of return flights on a private plane for up to 50 people, from London to Edinburgh, departing London City Airport on 1 June 2013 and returning on 2 June 2013. The prize also includes accommodation at the Sheraton Grand Hotel & Spa, Edinburgh and an Edinburgh Pass for each passenger. Accommodation is on a shared double room basis. Breakfast is included at the hotel. No other meals are included. Travel insurance, transfers and spending money are not included. The winner will be able to choose up to 49 passengers and must provide a full list Friday 24 May 2013. No supplements will be required if total number of travellers is less than 50. One out of every two passengers must be over 18 and all passengers must have a valid passport. By entering, your entry automatically becomes content that may be published on standard.co.uk/BA and other relevant channels. The winning entry will be the favourite of the judging panel. Determination and decision of the judging panel shall be final and no promotional correspondence will be entered into. The winner will be contacted by email, telephone or direct message (if the entry was made via Twitter) by Tuesday 14 May 2013. If we are unable to contact you successfully by midday on Tuesday 14 May 2013 the prize will be awarded to another entrant. The prize is non-transferable and there is no cash alternative. When you respond, The Evening Standard Ltd may use your information to contact you with offers/ services of interest by email. Only one entry per person is permitted. Promoter: British Airways Ltd. IATA: 125. Usual promotion rules apply, see www.standard.co.uk/rules. For further information, please write to Customer Care, Room 203b, Evening Standard Limited, Northcliffe House, 2 Derry Street, London, W8 5TT.

Ray Hatcher and his wife my daughter Debra Stone both submitted the following poems:

As a family we'd all like to fly
British Airways our choice, that's no lie
10 years in the city they've now taken off
They've looked after the queen and even the Hoff
In the Sheraton Grand, we'd take our repass
In Edinburgh fair we'd have a day pass
A day trip to Scotland, that would be nifty
To take to the skies, our family of 50

*Raymond Hatcher*

## DEBRA'S WINNING SUBMISSION

There's me, & the hubby and 48 more,
Check in at City, head count at the door,
BA is the airline, the best by a mile
Private plane don't ya know! We're flying in style.

In Scotland we'll land, our big family clan,
Time all together, that is the plan,
Aunties & uncles & cousins galore
Edinburgh is the city for us to explore

The kids are all grown up, they got big so fast,
The whole lot of us together, we'll all have a blast

*Debra Stone*

## DEBRA'S OTHER SUBMISSION

*which came second in the competition*

There once was a family from Kent
Who holiday'd each year in a tent,
But They won Bas prize & took to the shies,
From City to Scotland they went.

One day its my dream, to whisk my family away
Some time altogether, a great holiday,
The kids are all growing, they got big fast,
With cousins & aunties, we'll have a blast.

*Debra Stone*

# THE PRIZE

The memories we'll have,
The moments we'll treasure
BA, City & Scotland we love you forever.

# CONCLUSION

If death reveals the profundity of life
Then I am heading in the right direction.

# INDEX

Age 85
An Anatomy of Idiosyncrasies 129
An Earthly Life Begins 23
And Yet I Love Her 46
Ants 65
Ants Again 67
Astral Nightmare 42
Atomic Poem Three 69
Atomic Poem Two 49

Beauty of Lebanon, The 109
Beggar's Dog, A 125
Bizarre Thoughts 102
British Airways poems: 159

Clarity with Death 74
Clearness of Vision 56
Concrete Poem 1: The Paper Boy 105
Concrete Poem 2: Farewell Departed Wife and Friends 106

Dead Fishes 63

End of an Earthly Life, The 25
Epitaph 59

Fog Telegraphy 77
For Danielle 93
For Eileen 94
For Mary Ann (A Child) 51
For My Young Friend Monika 26
For the Dead Poets and Others 87
Foreigner, The 84
Forty Odd Years On 17
Futility 57

Ghost Lights 73
God Is a Nigger 95

Haunted 28
Home Sweet Home 113
Homosexual Temptation 68

I Am Alone 27
I Saw a Sad Dog! 126
Imprisoned 66

Lament of a Young Poet 91
Lebanon Inspired Poems
   by Bill Stone 117–29
   by Yasmin Hussein 107–15
Life Is a Kaleidoscope 44
Like a Stone 115

Mary Jane 96
Maybe? 128
Meaning of Life, The 114
Message for a Child 98
Minute Penned Thoughts 54
Modern Poetry 83
Movie 90
My Dog 48

Not So Grim Reaper, The 131

Palestine 35
Plain or Cheese and Onion? 76
Pleading for Recognition 45
Poem 1 99
Poem 2 99
Poem 3 100
Poem 4 100
Poem 5 101
Poem 6 101
Poem for the Freedom from Hunger Campaign, A 64
Poet at the Crucifixion, A 50

Poet Said It, A 43
Poet's Denunciation, A 53

Question, A 72

Respectful Reply to Dom
 Silvester Houédard 70

Sandman, The 112
Secrets 110
Shadow, The 88
Sick Humour? 124
Slow Is the Snail 127
Summer Rose, The 52

That's All Now Folks 151
This Ghost 30
Train Ride, The 116
This Moth 31
Thoraya 37
Thoughts 123
Thoughts in a Chinese
 Restaurant 92
Thoughts on Christmas Day 119
Two Concrete Poems 104

Untitled Lebanon Poems 120
Untitled Poems 99

Virgin and the Shadow, The 41
Visitors 32
Voice, The 111

Watching 75
Writing Then Is Like Talking 58

Years Later... 89

# A FERAL CAT DIES IN BEIRUT

## Bill Stone

A remarkable book full of insight, very well written and entertaining. In fact one of the best books I have read this year.

Phillip Bergersen – *Guardian Review Supplement*

I would like to recommend *A Feral Cat Dies in Beirut* (Gwenstone Publications) by Bill Stone. A strange, unsettling read, but highly entertaining.

*Reader's Digest* 'best literary discoveries of the year' recommendation

Printed in Great Britain
by Amazon